THE OXYGEN CYCLE

by Golriz Golkar

The Child's World®
childsworld.com

Published by The Child's World®
1980 Lookout Drive • Mankato, MN 56003-1705
800-599-READ • www.childsworld.com

Photographs ©: Shutterstock Images, cover
(foreground), 1 (foreground), cover (background),
1 (background), 6, 9, 20 (background), 20
(man and dog), 20 (right tree); Greg Brave/
Shutterstock Images, 5; Yurchanka Siarhei/
Shutterstock Images, 11; iStockphoto, 12, 15,
17; Federico Rostagno/iStockphoto, 18

ISBN 9781503828490
LCCN 2018944813

Printed in the United States of America
PAO2396

About the Author

Golriz Golkar is a teacher and children's
book author who lives in Nice, France. She
enjoys cooking, traveling, and looking for
ladybugs on nature walks.

Table of Contents

CHAPTER ONE

How the Cycle Works

Oxygen is an important **element** for life on Earth. It is a colorless and odorless gas. It makes up approximately 21 percent of Earth's **atmosphere**. Oxygen is constantly being created and used in different ways.

The oxygen cycle occurs between plants and animals in the biosphere. The biosphere is the part of Earth's crust, waters, and atmosphere that supports life. During **photosynthesis**, plants use sunlight to produce energy. They absorb sunlight using a green matter in their leaves called chlorophyll. The chlorophyll is used to combine a gas called carbon dioxide with water to make a sugar called glucose. The glucose is then used for the plant's **respiration**. It may also be changed into a starch and stored for later use.

Plants are a source of oxygen on Earth. ▶

During photosynthesis, plants produce oxygen. Plants release some of this oxygen into the atmosphere. This extra oxygen is used by animals and humans for respiration. During animal respiration, oxygen is inhaled and carbon dioxide is produced. Animals exhale this carbon dioxide back into the atmosphere. Plants use this carbon dioxide during their respiration, and the cycle continues.

Animals, including dogs, need oxygen to breathe.

Oxygen is also important for **decomposition**. When animals and plants die, bacteria break them down. The tiny life-forms release proteins called enzymes to break down the matter and absorb its nutrients. Certain bacteria use oxygen. Then they release carbon dioxide back into the atmosphere through respiration. Oxygen is needed for photosynthesis and decomposition to run smoothly. The oxygen cycle helps life on Earth remain balanced.

Most bacteria are tiny and can only be seen with a microscope.

TENSION

9

CHAPTER TWO

Oxygen in the Air and Water

Oxygen can combine with nearly any other element to make a new **compound**. Carbon dioxide is one example. It is made up of oxygen and carbon.

The ozone layer is also formed by oxygen. Ozone is essential to life on Earth. It acts as a shield protecting Earth's surface from the sun's harmful rays. Without ozone, humans and animals would be more likely to develop health issues, such as skin cancer and vision problems. Scientists worry about the ozone in the atmosphere being reduced. This reduction is caused by human activities.

The sun's powerful rays are dangerous, but the ozone layer helps protect people.

For example, spray-can products contain harmful chemicals. When the chemicals are released into the air, they are exposed to the sun's rays. A chemical reaction takes place, and ozone is broken down. Reducing air pollution is one way to protect the ozone in the atmosphere.

The most important compound oxygen makes is water. Life could not exist without it. Water is made from one oxygen **atom** and two hydrogen atoms. Bodies of water on Earth include glaciers and water vapor. The algae found in bodies of water generate most of the oxygen on Earth. They do this through photosynthesis. These algae replace about 90 percent of the oxygen used by living things all over the planet.

Glaciers are a form of solid water.

Oxygen also dissolves in water. This is needed for fish and other marine animals to breathe. Oxygen enters bodies of water through diffusion, or being pushed into the water from the atmosphere. It is also found in water when plants in the water release it during photosynthesis. Rising global temperatures and pollution are reducing oxygen in some ocean zones. Some marine animals cannot survive in these areas. If this continues to happen, many marine animals and plants could possibly die out.

Dolphins live in the ocean, but they need to surface to breathe air.

CHAPTER THREE
Oxygen in Earth's Crust

A lot of oxygen is present in Earth's crust. There is actually more oxygen in the crust than in the atmosphere. Oxygen is the most plentiful element found in the crust. Within rocks, oxygen cannot be easily separated from other elements. This is why the oxygen found in the crust is not useful for animals. Oxygen is not in its pure form. It cannot be used for life processes such as breathing.

Earth's crust also contains energy-rich materials. Some of these are **fossil fuels**. They are formed from the remains of plants and animals. People burn these fuels, such as coal, to create energy. When fossil fuels are burned, carbon dioxide is released into the atmosphere. Too much carbon dioxide makes Earth's climate warmer. It also makes ocean water more acidic. This is dangerous for marine animals.

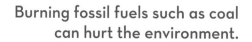
Burning fossil fuels such as coal can hurt the environment.

Oxygen and Fire

Fire needs oxygen to start. During **combustion**, a fuel is combined with oxygen to begin a fire. Earth's atmosphere is made of about 21 percent oxygen. This amount is perfect for combustion. If the atmosphere had less than 15 percent oxygen, fires could not start. At more than 25 percent oxygen, even wet material would burn easily.

Deforestation, or the cutting down and burning of trees, reduces Earth's oxygen levels. When there are fewer trees, less oxygen is produced through photosynthesis. Also, more carbon dioxide is left in the atmosphere.

Protecting the environment is important. Some scientists say that developments in farming are helping steady atmospheric oxygen levels. For example, vertical farming allows people to grow more plants in cities on the sides of skyscrapers! The world needs enough oxygen to support life on Earth.

Thousands of plants grow on the outside of a skyscraper in Milan, Italy.

The Oxygen Cycle

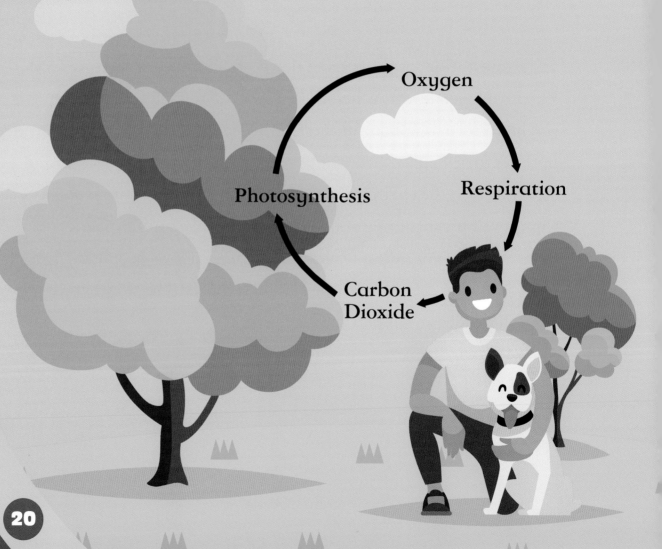

Oxygen

Respiration

Photosynthesis

Carbon
Dioxide

Fast Facts

- Oxygen is needed for life on Earth. Oxygen is constantly being created and used in different ways.

- Plants make oxygen during photosynthesis and release some into the atmosphere. Animals inhale oxygen and exhale carbon dioxide. Plants use this carbon dioxide, and the cycle continues.

- Oxygen forms ozone. The ozone protects Earth's surface from the sun's harmful rays.

- Oxygen dissolves in water and helps marine animals breathe.

- Oxygen combines with materials in Earth's crust. There is a lot of stored oxygen in Earth's crust.

- Deforestation and the burning of fossil fuels reduce Earth's oxygen supply.

Glossary

atmosphere (AT-muhs-feer) The atmosphere is the gases surrounding Earth. The atmosphere is made up of about 21 percent oxygen.

atom (AT-uhm) An atom is the basic building block of all matter. Water has one oxygen atom.

combustion (kuhm-BUS-chun) Combustion is the act or process of burning. A fire is an act of combustion.

compound (KAHM-pound) A compound is a substance that's created by combining two or more things. Oxygen combines with other elements to form a new compound.

decomposition (dee-kom-puh-ZISH-un) Decomposition is the act or process of decaying. Bacteria break down organic matter during decomposition.

element (EL-uh-muhnt) An element is a substance that can't be broken down into a smaller substance. Oxygen is an element.

fossil fuels (FAH-suhl FYOO-uhlz) Fossil fuels are organic materials from dead organisms that may be burned. Oil and coal are fossil fuels.

photosynthesis (foh-toh-SIN-thi-sis) Photosynthesis is the process by which a plant uses sunlight to change water and carbon dioxide into food for itself. During photosynthesis, a plant produces glucose for food.

respiration (res-puh-RAY-shun) Respiration is the process of taking in oxygen and giving out carbon dioxide. Plants use glucose as part of their respiration process.

To Learn More

IN THE LIBRARY

Belton, Blair. *How Coal Is Formed*.
New York, NY: Gareth Stevens Publishing, 2017.

Dakers, Diane. *The Nitrogen Cycle*. New
York, NY: Crabtree Publishing, 2015.

Flounders, Anne. *Healthy Trees, Healthy Planet*.
South Egremont, MA: Red Chair Press, 2014.

ON THE WEB

Visit our Web site for links about the oxygen cycle:
childsworld.com/links

*Note to Parents, Teachers, and Librarians: We routinely verify our Web links to make
sure they are safe and active sites. So encourage your readers to check them out!*

Index

Suddenly, Santa spots the most important place of all:
"Are you ready for me to visit your home?"
he says with a hearty chuckle.

It's time to leave out a glass of milk and a plate of
sugar cookies, snuggle up in bed with
your favorite teddy, and *listen very closely...*

'Twas the night before Christmas,
when all through the house,
Not a creature was stirring,
not even a mouse;

The stockings were hung
by the chimney with care,
In hope that St. Nicholas
soon would be there.

You were nestled up all snug in your bed,
While visions of candy canes danced in your head.
And from Winona to Minneapolis, all across the map,
Children had settled down for a long winter's nap.

0 0 1

sleep~~s~~ until santa visits

MINNESOTA

When out on the street
there arose such a clatter,
You sprang from your bed
to see what was the matter.

Away to the window
you flew like a flash,
Tore open the curtains,
threw open the latch.

WELCOME TO
MINNESOTA
Santa

PLEASE
STOP
HERE

The moon in the sky
with its full winter glow,
Shone bright as midday
on Minnesota below.

When, what to your
wondering eyes should appear,
But a miniature sleigh
and eight tiny reindeer.

BEMIDJI
PAUL
BUNYAN
1937

With a little old driver,
so lively and quick,
You knew in a moment
it must be St. Nick.
More rapid than eagles
his reindeer they came,
And he whistled, and shouted,
and called them by name:

"Now, Dasher! Now, Dancer!
Now, Prancer and Vixen!
On, Comet! On, Cupid!
On, Donder and Blitzen!
Take me up to the chimney; follow my call!
Now dash away, dash away, dash away all!"

And then, in a twinkling,
you heard on the roof
The prancing and pawing
of each little hoof.

As you pulled in your head
and were turning around,
Down the chimney
St. Nicholas came with a bound.

He was dressed all in fur,
from his head to his foot,
And his clothes were all tarnished
with ashes and soot.
A bundle of toys he had
flung on his back,
And he looked like a peddler
holding his pack.

His eyes–how they twinkled!
His dimples–how merry!
His cheeks were like roses,
his nose like a cherry.
His droll little mouth
was drawn up like a bow,
And the beard on his chin was
as white as the snow.

Dear Santa,
Welcome back to
Minnesota!
I hope you enjoy the
yummy treats I have
left out for you.

Love from your
biggest fan!
xxx

He glanced at the names
that he held in his fist,
Children in Anoka and Saint Paul
whom were next on his list.
He had a broad face
and a little round belly
That shook when he laughed,
like a bowl full of jelly.

He was chubby and plump,
a right jolly old elf,
And you laughed when you saw him,
in spite of yourself.
St. Nick winked an eye
and tilted his head,
Letting you know
you had nothing to dread.

He spoke not a word,
but went straight to his work,
And filled up your stocking,
then turned with a jerk.

I ♥ MINNESOTA

And tapping his finger
at the side of his nose,
And giving a nod,

He sprang to his sleigh,
to his team gave a whistle,
And away they all flew
like the down of a thistle.
But St. Nicholas exclaimed,
as he drove out of sight—

THANK
YOU
Santa

Santa's magical journey is coming to an end.
He delivers the final gifts to Bloomington and St. Cloud,
waves goodbye to the 10,000 lakes, and laughs a
jolly *Ho-Ho-Ho* for everyone to hear.

Heading back home to his cozy workshop at the North Pole, Santa hopes each child is *extra* good next year...because he can't wait to come back to

Minnesota!

Adapted from the poem by Clement C. Moore
Illustrated by Jo Parry
Designed by Ryan Dunn

Copyright © Bidu Bidu Books Ltd. 2021

Published by Hometown World,
an imprint of Sourcebooks Kids
P.O. Box 4410, Naperville, Illinois 60567-4410
(630) 961-3900
hometownworld.com
sourcebookskids.com

Date of Production: May 2021
Run Number: 5020473
Printed and bound in China (OGP)
10 9 8 7 6 5 4 3 2 1

To ....

CONGRATULATIONS

We are **SUPER** excited to inform you that
you made it onto the **NICE LIST**.
Keep up the good work and remember
to always be **KIND** and **MERRY**.
You are **TRULY** special.

Love,

Santa

and the elves

xXx